ASPHALT SOUNDS

Dedicated to my husband Tonci, my daughters
Dana and Adrienne, my parents Grace and Phil Arnaldi,
and in memory of the spirits of the Atlantic Ocean,
Adrienne and John Neuweiler.

ASPHALT SOUNDS

BY DENISE KOLANOVIC

Cover Photograph
by Dave Green

FORE ANGELS PRESS

ISBN 0-9658920-5-0

Published by
FORE ANGELS PRESS
267 Woodbury Road
Huntington, NY 11743

introduction

When Christopher Marlowe alluded to "Nature that framed us of four elements" in TAMBURLAINE, he echoed an ancient doctrine that earth, water, air and fire, in various combinations, constitute our natural world. In Denise Kolanovic's ASPHALT SOUNDS, the reader encounters a poet who revels in the physical universe and is powerfully attracted to air and water.

The tone of the collection is set by its first two poems, "Girl Speaking to Maxfield Parrish's 'Ecstacy'," a celebration of air, and "Pisces and Man," a hymn to the sea. Parrish would have rejoiced in the lyric with which the book begins.

In "Illumination," water becomes a pathway to paradise. The author views her young sister as a "water nymph" in "The Spirit of Peggy's Cove". In "Croatia," a complex piece in which some Croatian words occur, she extols water as an escape from "hellish heat". In "Ancient Rose," an evocative poem that implies more than it states, she invites the reader to hear the "swirling songs" of water.

Although the author uses free verse in most of her work, she knows how to compose in metrical form. She has an ear for rhythm which prevents her free verse from crumbling into prose.

Air and water are connected with a personal tragedy from which the poet may never recover. Still, she celebrates those elements as inexhaustible sources of physical and spiritual renewal.

Dr. Alfred Dorn, June 15, 2004

Acknowledgments:

"An Infinite Journey", "Ceilidh", "Eve's Legacy", "Eve's Legacy Adam's Apple", "Goodrichie", "Silver Wings", "The Pen Woman", National League of American Pen Women, Inc.

table of contents

preface

This book of poems is in memory of my sister and brother-in-law who, on September 2, 1998, were randomly aboard Swissair Flight 111 on their way to Greece to celebrate their 10th wedding anniversary. The plane crashed into the Atlantic Ocean near the shores of Nova Scotia within one hour of flight time. Over two hundred human beings were killed along with Adrienne and John.

This is unfathomable and horrible. The only way to move on is to go through the agony of not understanding why things like this happen. Of course, it is very hard to look death in the face and to say to yourself, "Yes, eventually this is my destiny." In poetry, the concept of death appears frequently. Many poets have visited this dark place because it is as fascinating as it is frightening. But the beauty of poetry is that it can get you through fear. It uses metaphor to explain rainbows, heavens and hells.

Many of us have experienced intuitive moments when it seemed as though the universe asserted itself and linked us to eternity. This is intuition. Walt Whitman said that poetry is revisiting a memory charged with emotion. That charge is intangible, yet it is real. It causes goosebumps. It causes the heart to race or slow down.

The poems in this book are a compilation of more than twenty-five years of thinking, living, losing and loving. They are my attempts to crystalize my world. I am thankful to my publisher and friend, Anna Di Bella, for making my dream a reality.

girl speaking to maxfield parrish's "ecstasy"

Swirling clouds call to me.
Tiptoeing to the edge, I wrap
my arms around myself.

Now is the moment.

There is no other blue
but for the sky right now,
bathed in salmon and gold.

I am free. I can fly,
my scarves blowing,
chaining my body.

O, sweet wind and dusty
rock, lift me to infinity!
Lift me in an eternal stroke
of your brush.

pisces and man

Blue and green pools of water surround fish
which swim and live in flowing air. They must
know something which humans cannot fathom.
Deep in the earth lives the secret of time
stretching in the void of hollow wishes
and metal rock, breaking and melting
everything that lies below the continents.
Fish must fathom time-wishes!

But what do fish know?
The urchins and sleek eels
slither and sneak beyond the gully cave.
The whales and dolphins sing
ancient chants of alien survival.
Salmon swim sideways upstream, frenzied,
uncontrolled, toward their purpose, then death.
Eels cave-sing survival.

But what do humans know
swimming in watery uteruses?

the catsnake dream

You used to be a she cat with emerald eyes
and a serpentine tail that would slink through
soot, dark alleys and cheshire smiles.
Your teeth would sink into the throats of swallows.
You kneaded through their wings to form
a blanket as you purred yourself to sleep.

But now you are a snake.
Your surreptitious skin molts old scales.
You lurch across arid rocks.
Your yellow eyes watch your fangs
as you smile lies.
You sleep with your eyes open.

seachange

Washing in the waves.
Washing in the water.
It has happened.
It is happening again.

"O, lift me out of this!"

But there is no body here anymore.
There is only sea softness.

Don't you know
that you are changing
into foam and salt
and
tiny willy nilly sea urchins
and little lobsters?

And you are
truthing.
It's time to move on.

"Lift me out of this!"

You are changing, sweetly now, softly.
Of course, you could not have known
what was happening to you.
Look up.

"I have no eyes!"

But now you can see.

verrazano bridge

When the sky and sun merge
just before dusk
into gunmetal gray
and clouds look like
fish bones mirrored
in the sea,
I am glad to be part
of the bridge.
Its bright grayness,
except for one enormous
orange ball
which extends for miles,
is all there is for me.

mirror meditation

I see the world upsidedown in a glass
but discern the image from the object.
One is a single dimension, the other is mass.
My eyes are part of me. I am the subject.

I gaze at a mirror and perceive a face
I know is mine, and I rest at ease.
I am glad to be here in this time and place.
I have taken my head out of deep freeze.

I thaw and I become supple and warm.
Each day flips pages in my diary
of life, where love and peace slowly transform
my mind to write my world with imagery.

ego villanelle

Are you special as you gaze in the mirror?
What do you see? Can it really be you?
If you bang the glass, does your face quiver?

When racing to catch a train do you ever
push and shove him or her over there, too?
Are you special as you gaze in the mirror?

Do you stare into space and watch the world shiver
as winter winds sweep frozen tears? Do you?
If you bang the glass does your face quiver?

Would you poison your own healthy liver
because you don't care anymore? It's come due.
Are you special as you gaze in the mirror?

And see your plump sideview from the sliver
stuffed inside yourself, undigested rue?
If you bang the glass, does your face quiver?

Do you draw curtains around the lever
like "Oz" did, while a god hiding from view?
Are you special as you gaze in the mirror?
If you bang the glass, does your face quiver?

aphrodite's love song to hippolytus

Oh, Hippolytus, why do you praise another?
You swore your love to me and yet I hear
Your Song to Artemis, the Maiden Goddess.
This accolade to her explodes my ear.

Why do you sway from me, ignore my flame,
my power which transformed you once
into perfect blue heat and erotic pleasure?
Has she made you her prey for childish hunts?

You sing now to your virgin sorceress.
Hippolytus, you will not escape from time.
Do not assume strength comes from youth
or innocence. No, it is your intrinsic sign.

Come back to me, your passion and your depth
shall filter through my divinity.
You will remember my love and become
again my own, for all eternity

trojan woman

Euripides, your women suppressed
their longings and white wishes
to savage love and jealous-raging war.

They cluster around
crying in chorus.
Polyxena was sacrificed
and so was the sublime.
They rotate and revolve
like worker bees,
mimicking activity.

They wail:
Hail, Andromache, singing
the songs of mourning
in black rags, of glory gone
and the hideous, here.

Learning there is no forgiveness
in tragedy, nor forgetting,
we become the hanging-on hags
who watch new wars waged.

someday love *(for tonci)*

Far away in another land we kiss.
Drawing in the breath
our eyes meet and stare
to dream the dream
we made to share.
I touch your face.
My fingers speak to me
in breathless sighs.
You touch my hand
and lip-brush
my pulsing vein...
gently.
I faint slowly and you gather
me in your arms withdrawing
my frightened hair from my brow.
Heavy lids testify
my fear of nakedness.
Sweetly, you nestle my
head upon your thumping chest
and I rub my nose against your rib.
Come fly to me.
Do not blink your busy eyes clear.
Come to me from my dream.
For words were planted,
"run to me,"
inside my soul.

thorns on rosebushes

Peeking through a rosebush
I see you standing between
the thorn and salmon-rose.
The scent is extraordinary.
But no one grows roses anymore:
all that water, pruning,
their temperamental natures.

Impatiens.
They're everywhere,
all budded and bushy,
odorless.
Every year you laugh
as I replant them.

to wordworth's "ode: intimations on immortality I"

I have dreamed the same dream as you:
infants born of heaven's bliss
waking into the nightmare of human nature,
droplets of truth drying each day into the bleakness of life.

Unlearning the knowledge of angels, we learn to cry.
Only in dreaming do we remember
what we've forgotten, the soul's memory
fringing vision of the closed eye and our
humming minds mingling with the devil's lie.

But so be it, and it is relinquished, once known.
Then the poet need not imagine a heaven so far off
or a heaven lost forever, save innocence.

For that keeps the lie alive, that nothing is fair.
I have dreamed the same dream as you
and I reincarnate my vision from yours
with but a few changes.

to wordworth's "ode: intimations on immortality II"

Once when midnight came to break all dreams
of silver wishes, love lights and the like,
a man did stop the hour with such schemes
that are uncommon to such folk who hike
the hills. The witching twelve did strike
that eve, and all who slept had no recall
of time or their realities at all.

This man of wit and strength recorded beams,
joy sounds and chords of umbilical light.
Blazing smoke did strip the air and seal the seams
as twilight turned to dawn, just as a poet's might
may hold the waters back. A human psyche
can dream all night and altered sight can fall
then rise, restoring to all dreamers glory's call.

to jim morrison

I hear your music:
electronic pipe organ,
an artist's frustrated scream.
I read your words
swollen with drugs.
You are not a sober poet.
Oh, Banshee lover,
worshipper of Dionysus
the two-faced god,
abundant harvester and drunken lecher,
you crossed the thin line
between genius and depravity.

I read the biographic interpretations
of your Indian Shaman.
Were they accurate?
Did you ever want peace and love?

You are not answering.

Are you free of your body machine?
Is Anne with you? Or Sylvia or Jimi
or Virginia?

What is worth the legacy of
drunken bouts and inflamed ego?
What is worth the temptation?

What can we learn
who remain in L'america,
who remain on this wounded earth
you left behind?
What can we learn?

You are not answering.

You had a yearning to open doors,
even with bloody fingertips.
Doors to where?
Where, after all, can a soul go?

joy dancing: echoes of edgar allan poe

Something wonderful will happen
when your fingers begin snapping
and your feet proceed to tapping
to a beat that you can hear.

It's in rhythm with the clapping
of the waves and with the flapping
of the gull wings which are mapping
passage to their summer pier.

TIme is now and time is lasting
and the past is gently passing
as the people go on dancing
to the beat that they can hear.

It's the dance of now, forever.
It's the joy of an endeavor
to be free in timeless splendor
in the moment that is here.

snowcap archaic villanelle

The snow upon the summit shines so white.
I breathe the freshness in the air so pure,
run up and catch a glimpse of Heaven's light.

A seagull cry has called to some whose sight
waits patiently aware and calmly sure.
The snow upon the summit shines so white.

As ships on sea-dark waves imploring sight
from lighthouse beams that guide them back to shore,
run up and catch a glimpse of Heaven's light.

Join hands and dance as diamond stars beam bright,
illuminating hearts that gladly roar,
"The snow upon the summit shines so white!"

A piper plays a tune that does invite
all men who wish to heal and then to cure,
run up and catch a glimpse of Heaven's light.

O, happy men, who seek eternal height,
proclaim these words of peace forevermore:
"The snow upon the summit shines so white.
Run up and catch a glimpse of Heaven's light."

mount kilimanjaro

I see your snow peak,
feel the cold wetness
numbing my face.
My mouth salivates now.
Heat and coldness cause
blood to redden my cheeks.
The extremes produce the same.
Hermetic.
Opposites, degrees, vibrations,
genders, polarities.
Remembering all things are the same,
I forget.

I see your vastness.
Merging with your image,
I feel comfort
and a chilling sensation.

I wish to extend myself
into cold wetness,
height beyond height,
daring myself to
reach my summit.

continental drifting

The mountains are moving!
The mountains have moved.

Falling into fire sea they clutch
the earth and flow down quickly,
red hot and glowing, down, down
into the valleys.
A fire gaucherie, a molten hellfire
gushed the plain land,
transforming the horizon
into quick-glossed hardpan.

The storm-puddled lava
spits lies and gossip.
The storm-puddled lava,
a sore under mantle and bedrock,
breaks the core.

gertrude on the grass *(for gertrude ryder bennett)*

She paints life with an amber brush.
Liquid love flows simply. There is one choice:
to see clouds or sun. The grass is very plush
in the garden. Birded wind is the voice
that directs her encounter on a plush
carpet threaded with golds and reds. Her voice
unifies color with sound via brush
in a loose hand. She has one silver choice:
to be a woman, bird-flying in plush
aqua-air with straw hat, focusing her voice
beyond the atmosphere, her fluted voice.
She transforms cotton to warm, plush
wool. She is an alchemist with a brush.

mother and child

We are linked.
You wired into me long ago
when grass seedlings were planted
by the chutes of daffodils, hyacinth and roses.
Then you were not you, nor was I, I.
But we were then, you and I,
measured in white light,
in purple air.

winter

The north wind's song taps glass and rips weak trees.
Moving fast and swifty, it moves harsh, bitter air
creating a vacuum, an empty space dispelling all things
in its way. "Move along! Let me come through!"
A few old birds hold fast, clinging to corners,
narrow wind sills and white steel gutters.
Their cracked wings display tiny holes and scars
where feathers used to be. They huddle
in a tribunal, to combat the incessant wind.
A few black leaves, like onyx jewels,
singletons, glitter garish trees,
remembrance of another time,
when green warmth was reality
and breezes softly blew.

echoes in heaven

Pure silk and satin clothe
the smiling, loving, soft people.
Only the very best for them.
Not through greed or self-indulgent
screams do they acquire things.
They merely display their
rightful inheritance.
They are contented kings
in harmony with the universe.
They move together
like two leaves bonding,
becoming a sturdy stem.
They glow like hot coals
and rest from dark and ancient
threats of fire.
They make smooth sounds in the night
that echo in heaven.

evening breath:
a response to "to a skylark" by percy bysshe shelley

The young, green trees
of early spring:
their leaves are formed in childish splendor
frail and thin against
evening's dark renders.
They loom overhead
with arms outspread
as if to sing aloud,
"How sweet to float in night's cool tender."

The silent thunder
bellows miles away,
in waves that will pave lightning
and streak the sky with slanting dew.
And still the evening is
the leaves,
closing center veins
till light of morning
implores them to open wide,
green against the breathing navy sky.

for percy bysshe shelley

You were a ball of light in motion,
ever changing into energy, limitless.
Eternal love sang in your
whipping words with rhythms
vibrating into high music.
You transformed life into ecstasy.

Your henna curls played softly
on your face like crested waves
against sharp marble stones.

You danced in wondrous whirlpools
breaking the ocean's symphony.

You succumbed recklessly
to your enchanted journey,
surrendering your life with Ariel.
You designed your destiny,
patterning your days rebelliously.

Mingling with the siren's scream,
you summoned death.
You listened and you followed
their every breath.

genesis

Please forgive me
for loving you,
for opening my soul
to your heart
and letting you see
my nakedness.

Please do not punish me
with worthless wrangling
and angry kisses.

The morning star still
succumbs to the sun
as I to you,
soft and tender
as a sea breeze.

Adam, it was your
first stare that caused
my pupils to dilate
in the garden.

the submissive and sublime lady
after robert browning's "my last duchess"

He liked to frame my features.
He liked to frame my soul,
as if he could, the old vulture.
Pussyfooting, I did. I had to.
He pushed me into corners and
then would kiss me and tell me,
when we were alone: "Baciami amore mio."

Yes, yes, I will kiss your misogynist mouth,
your mustache waxed and neatly curled.

He hated my virtues:
that I loved so easily,
that I was SO easy,
that I was so easily taken,
without him, so pathetically nothing.

He liked to throw daisies to the floor,
watch me crawl to pick them up.
He liked to watch me grovel
and delighted in my tears.

My Duke, my Italian tyrant,
called me Criseyde but I was
more like Penelope and when
I realized he was Bluebeard
it was too late.

the harvester

She raised her raven skirt, curtsied the land.
The dark, rich earth gave birth once again
and thin grey rats sniffed her sweet soiled hand.
She shooed them away like a harpy hen.
Fast they did scurry past her full garden
of yellow wax squash waiting to be reaped.
Plump round pumpkins sat ripe in rows of ten
and golden corn, still mummied, shyly peeped
to find their Autumn Princess. And they leaped
as proud heroes to be chosen for that night
in splendor; their lives, gifts rendered complete.
She dried her brow, welcoming the new light
that summons the seed dreams of fruitful life.
She joined the sun, with one kiss, as its wife.

the banquet

The harvest was good this year
and so I gather them to feed
together - at a wooden table - dear,
sweet table - solid and warm.

Brothers, gather round with the wine
that my toes kissed, a purple sign
of love.

The bread with living yeast
fulfils our bellies for this feast.
It satisfies.

Something whispers to us:
"The dreamer plants its seed
before the dawn, before the deed.
The dreamer makes the meal complete,
preparing bread from stalks of wheat."

joint power

She cried because she lived behind a wall:
sometimes a woman, displaced, without a role.
It burned her hidden center, made her call:
a shriek-scream, black and dead as pressured coal.

It took away her babies, took them all.
It also took her body, mind and soul.
Each day became a battle not to fall
or eat through earth like a senseless mole.

How can she heal her dark,
disheartened life? With joy-dreams dancing
a flight of diamond wings.
Creation's light, a brilliant spark,
is a crystalline life that spins,
linking two beings
as joint-power kings.

illumination

Children of the Universe, your sight is restored.
Return to your home in the happy dream.
The kingdom lies there.
Listen to the ancient calling.
The star rises in your eastern eyes
this navy night, shedding light between sun
and moon where a pastel rainbow
bridges the gap of separation.

Walk along in wonder and scatter your
diamond seeds to reap instant innocence.
Unleashed eagles will fly from
your jewelled crowns and kiss the great
dove waiting on the shore.
You will bathe in waters of truth
streaming in surrender
back to the source.

Dive and be baptised after your
weary sojourn.
Refreshed in love at last,
return to paradise.

empowerment

The universe is my happy kingdom.
It says yes to all requests I ask of it.
No matter what the thing is that I want.

Its optimism is life-affirming,
abundant, rich, something I treasure.
And all I have to do it call upon it.

The universe is my happy kingdom.
I am free to climb the hills and cross its roads.
I am thrilled to hold a leaf and then to swim.

Its optimism is life-affirming.
There are no boundaries and yet I know
where I must travel without second thought.

My universe is my happy kingdom,
and all the places to which I travel
are exactly where I am meant to be.

It optimism is life-affirming.
The universe always says yes, yes, yes.
Even stumblings are part of my path.

The universe is my happy kingdom.
There is no doubt along two-poled roads.
Both sides merge into one, and when I
stop labelling the poles as good or bad,
the universe is my happy kingdom.
Its optimism is life-affirming.

the damned robot:
a response to "the man with the hoe" by edwin markham

He thinks he must break his back
to repay his sin of birth
separate from the sun and blind
to dreams of stars.
He squints his eyes
creating crevices between his brows.
Relief:
a yawn, a drink or smoke.
He snaps the trance of routine labor
until sleep comforts.

Then, chained by tradition,
he burrows in his tunnel,
away from the light.

He hates the night,
but veiled in nightmared vision,
he worships its unknown blackness.

He expects crumbs to satisfy his hunger.
And, if by chance, he thinks a slice
of leavened bread should come instead,
he will rejoice like a pagan.

a ripple effect *(for virginia bagliore)*

Your eyes burn my core
like phosphorus fireflies.
And now, light torches,
they illuminate soul dancers in space,
setting first causes into effect.

Transcending
flesh and pain,
you fell into Love's lap
where all energy is
once removed,
a sun change,
perfect.

Intrepid source of white vibration,
jump the planes of iridescent infinity
and in lavender sleep
become the wind and lift me.

soul within a soul *(for anna di bella)*

When the poet becomes the poem
which poem will it be:

Pastoral roads on which to roam
or dark depths of the sea?

Choose your words. Your images comb
the surfaces of dreams.

And if you fall into the poem,
save your self-prophecy.

american butterfly

Always moving, wings go flitter,
flutter up and down. She is found
in constant motion: ajitter.
The butterfly ate a bitter
root which drove her up and down:
always moving, wings go flitter.
She darts. Hunters cannot hit her
as she dances but makes no sound,
in constant motion: ajitter
And in the chilling air of winter,
she does not stand still. Wings are
always moving, wings aflitter.
She dances as bluebirds twitter,
a ritual on sacred ground.
In constant motion: ajitter,
twitching to a beat. Is she a duck-sitter?
No. She is freedom-bound.
Always moving, wings aflitter,
in constant motion: ajitter.

a subtle lobotomy

She walks along the littered city streets.
Her face is slightly bloated; eyes are staring
as she steps up to a counter bearing
pastries. She is an old child buying treats.
Her hunger is so deep, although she eats
sugar and bread to stop the glaring
emptiness. She blocks the world's uncaring
with a sweet. She deprives herself of meat.

Her coat is ragged. She was abandoned,
and now she lives in an economy
she does not understand. She does not see.
Her ghost-thoughts make her laugh and she is shunned.
A taxi nearly hits her. She is stunned.
She does not understand. She floats by me.

from dante's inferno

I have entered a nightmare
from which I cannot awaken.
I cannot escape its thick trees
or denseness of insane thoughts
with no constraints of time.

Without liquid movement
or a voice or a sense of time
there is no freedom from this swamp.
I am motionless.
I am motionless in a reverie
among perfumed pine needles.

Dark greenness suffocates
my lungs. I cannot awaken.
The sap has locked my lips
and I mumble some inane thought,
dreading the denseness.

My hands push/pull directing my eyes.
Pine needles stick under my nails.
I crawl through the dark denseness.
Time is mouthstickly thick,
gaggingly sweet.

I have no voice, I feel no time.
This strange denseness
has become my own forest,
my dark mystery. My forest
does not allow me to awaken.

I pass the decaying treestumps.
I break one of Jocasta's branches.
She is locked in your hell-forest too,
bleeding because that IS her voice.
She is motionless, silenced
by the dark, green denseness.

I am a tree in my forest.
I am a reverie
which cannot awaken.

letter to my wife: a reply to ezra pound's translation of "the river merchant's wife"

I dreaded to leave you alone.
So perfect was your face that day
as you forced a smile
of acceptance.
This memory sustained me when
Ku-to-yen devoured me whole.

I came back then but left many times more.
Each time one tear, scraping your cheek,
was spread invisible
as you laughed lowly.
I, too, measure time with nature.
I know storms are building when
small animals clean behind their ears.

Many storms have formed
and are forgotten.
But the blue-green water of Kiang
will not have me wading
through to find you.
Do not look for me at Cho-fu-sa.
But let me fly to you
from the clouds.
When I land
I will
run faster than light
into your wanting arms.

buddha at cho-fu-sa

Their eyes slant slightly and golden beams
link to mine through wind
and we are one again.
As I gaze up
at You in the hold of sky,
clouds pardon themselves of Your splendor.
Your glowing streams of light
raise me to greet You, releasing me of them.
My heart, below my head,
beats in Your embrace
until I know I am with You.
I know I am.
I know.
I am.

yoga poem

I sit on a silent lotus blossom
atop the murky lake and breathe deep breaths;
I hide below the petals I've become.

In contemplation pray Sakti, come!
Plant your seeds serene of snow-white rest.
I sit on a silent lotus blossom.

Bacchus smiles, his amber chalice of rum
at hand. He offers me a sip. Perplexed,
I hide below the petals I have become.

the first chakra

The Divine Mother Sakti cups your spine.
As you stretch and breathe you release
darknesses locked between your bones.
Each move brings you closer to your fears.
When you bend and breathe, you can feel.

And when you breathe, you can smell her odors.
She is not leaping on red and gold tapestry pillows
as your earthly guru suggested.
You try to see her but only envision an Indian prototype.

When you sun-worship or become a corpse
or sit cross-legged with your fingertips making an "o",
you may glimpse her indigo vestments.
You check your fingertips for white light emissions
as she cups your kundalini spine.

Whenever fear is present
or whenever you forget what you are,
your electric fingers remind you that you are safe.
Unkinking the spine is dangerous
some have told you.

But the Divine Mother Sakti, wearing indigo,
balances red and blue.
With her white words she guides your journey
through sun fires and black snakes,
allowing you to align your strong, strong spine.

eclipse

The sun rose up and the night disappeared
and its rays were warm as they dried up tears
that the grass had wept while the moon just leered
when the sun rose up

The sun burst big and it sizzled streets
and shades did a dance where the river meets.
The cool, dry breeze made neat rippled pleats
as the sun burst big.

The sun turned rust and it melted down
while the sky buried blue on the tired town.
But the people sang while underground
when the sun turned rust.

The sun slipped past the edges of sight
until blue-black air scattered dots of white
to shine sweetened grace in lieu of light
as the sun slipped past.

north wind prayer

The pain drills. The sound is a nightmare.
I see black and red, blood everywhere.
I cry knives.

I look back; it looks bright as I dare
in mindless contemplation to stare.
The pain drills.

In slow-motion darkness I am aware
of cold hands that nail-scratch, rip me and tear.
I cry knives.

Thunder bursts opaque clouds to break down air
that rains on a desert, scorched and bare.
The pain drills.

The sky sags as wind moves through the air.
Through branches, it whispers, "North Wind Prayer".
I cry knives.

I plead for a pure sound to repair
the hums and hollers deep in my ear.
And then I remember my North Wind Prayer.

no time to waste *(to shelley and byron)*

Transcendentalists leave reality
in lieu of
Idealism,
Artistic Purity,
Utopia,
Anarchy.

You did not touch American
soil. But it did not remain soil.
Perfect, positive rhythms
control nothing
because we are water.

Return, return to the sea
until it evaporates.
Return, return to the air
until it dissipates.
Return, return to the
microcosm of spirit
of which you wrote.

for dad

Your hands write cryptic numbers
linked to cards, a game you enjoy
but one I do not understand.
Now I see why you play so steadily,
beaming childhood into your repertoire of responsibility.
I smile when Yankee sounds
play in the background as you paint
the ground green with a thin brush.

You taught me the joy of words
and the fun of puns.
If I only had learned Italian,
it would have come full circle to
the pisan circle of Giovanni
on the isle of Elba, where
fig and olive trees swayed
far away from America

the fortunate fall

We've walked these streets before
curlicuing 41st and Park.
You and Ed stopped before me,
crossed the street,
said hello and walked on.
While I, in running pantyhose,
with my hem hanging,
a soiled coat unbuttoned
and dèjás vu,
could not hold my tears back.
Exposure: final.
My diary read and
reenacted by you.
No consequence.
No emancipation.
Just a silent mouthful of humiliation.

I am here again on 41st and Park,
the buildings shading blue skies.
Icy breezes cascade sidewalks,
whipping women's legs.
The vagrants and construction are still
marauding. The particulars are erased,
the essence of the double lines
the same.

But I, well-manicured and smiling,
am in a minivan.

f train

I missed my train.
Peering down the tunnel
I squinted.
Nothing in sight
along the black tracks
except rustling water
and two brown rats
scurrying the second rail.
Commuters paced.
I opened my book,
could not read.
I had to keep checking
the tunnel for that
glimmer.

spirit of peggy's cove

My little sister,
kiss me again, again.

I think of your dark hair,
straight nose and almond eyes.

My little sister,
when I call upon your memory
I can almost smell and feel
your soft skin and breath.

My thoughts now dance around you,
a water nymph, a muse
fragmenting my right brain.

Now we visit in dreams,
visions of sunflowers and
spontaneous consciousness

My little sister,
your essence is in my
Parrish paintings,
your Chinese bridges and
Italian vistas.

I see you between
the autumn princess and spring unicorn.
We'll kiss again,
again.

asphalt sounds

They speak to me in swirling vowels
la la la-ing the landscape
with white satin sheaths and wings.

Chanting, chanting:
the monk hems hit their sandals.
Chanting, chanting:
their somber hums exude deep man sounds
that balance darkness and lift the veil
revealing the metaphor.

I hear them in my sweet dreams.
They are in the asphalt.
Can they hear me when
I speak lavender words?

croatia

The air is hot and pure,
salty and satisfying.

The sea, More,
finally darks blue
after weeks of hellish heat
and layers of stagnant air.
"Vruće" they cry.

Yes, it is very hot. But today
my rosary is a litany
and I remember the reason why
I enjoy this village existence.
It is a vague memory
of honesty and hard work,
of wanting bleached white rock
and fresh fish.

I nap everyday. I have no choice.
I must sleep the heat away.
But my Turkish coffee
will wake me up.

The children are so alive here
on this fisherman beach.
There are no couches,
only soft waves, light brown sand
and clanking masts against the wind.

More: pronounced morra, means "sea" in Croatian
Vruće: pronounced vrucha; means "hot" in Croatian

the ladder

A sparkling silence spreads thickly in my mind:
a comforting blanket, etching designs
of streaming waters moving smooth and calm,
refracting sun's sword rays in neat straight lines
glowing red hot, then white as sequinned signs

This solar view becomes a sacred peace, like balm
upon my soul that calls on me to sing.
To find the crown and free the king
to reign again, which is my destiny.
The king inside of me, the king is me.

The ancient trees carry bird-tired wings,
a sanctuary rich in purity,
and sun by air restores and brings
the truth to shine, freedom from decay.

nightmare in 9 parts

I

It swoops down landing vertically.
It mingles with the state of things
in old earth.
Careless of time, it
waits, furrowing plans in slumber.
Glazed eyes dream of yellow wisps
and half images.

II

Fresh air dances
through lungs,
and feet walk buoyantly
with purpose.
Defiant of shadows,
meantimes or suppositions.
Now is always. Good.
And like blue skies, it really
is half true.

III

It taps against the window.
The wind is there:
Is it trying to enter without invitation?
Beggar!

IV

Hearing is not the same
at night when dream-screams
are branches against the window.
But no! Not now.
Shades are drawn.
The half images call.

V
Morning.
Light knows when to happen.
That is why dragons chase the chariot,
exploding stars and chipping hot rocks.
into diamond dots in black laughter.

VI
Exposure is its function,
to survive in the wooden slivers.
Wings are sedimented,
almost petrified now,
so slow and angry.
Energy is frozen but it must move.
So... try again, tonight.

VII
Twinkling light
comes in - moonlight -
gold blaze:
daze, daze.
morning sprinkles over
like marmalade sticking
sticking -
mouth-stretching, gagging
at corners.
Sweetness, sweetness.
Sleep.
Closing in.

VIII
Ah hem!
Nothing.
Wind dances tap.
What, what?
REM stops.

... up and up and up.
Zooming up and out.
Hmmmmmmmmmmmmmm.
Open window.
What is there?

IX
Morning again.
Sweetness?
O tired now.
So weak now.
The veins absorbing, somehow,
gold, warm liquid.

isadora

You wore a long scarf
and danced with arms flailing.
You liked to move slowly
like a ship sailing.
You made an art
of leaf dancers
hovering across ice ground.
You were graceful
and frenetic swirling
chiffon
cloth-forms
radiating the ice,
fire-coating your eyes,
your scarf, the chain.

duality

Black pearl rolls
in white water,
never, never goes under.

Black pearl bowls
like thud-thunder
down, down alleys.

Black pearl calls
white pearl the martyr.
Far off in valleys.

Black pearl pierces the peace
in half, in half.
Why, why, black pearl?

the unicorn

The Unicorn stays in its circle yard.
All flowers, nature's beauty, are its guard.
It sleeps in white blossoms of baby's breath
awaiting the dawn, unafraid of death.

The Unicorn stays certain within its fence.
It dreams of peace and love and innocence.
When stars come through and darkness hides the light
the Unicorn alone divines its sight.

It dreams of peace and love as hands touch hands.
It thinks of miracles in distant lands.
It breathes forgiveness, purifying pain.
It travels to hearts, ideas free of blame.

They say it is extinct, mere myth or tale
from Medieval times when men wore steel
to guard their breasts from death, men who pierced peace
and stabbed the Unicorn, the pascal fleece.

And still the Unicorn rules its domain
between the pink and silver dots of rain.
Beyond horizon, vision unmarred,
the Unicorn stays in its circle yard.

hormone therapy

I'll pop a pill and dye my hair
or get a tuck, buy underwear.
I have to be fifteen again.
I want to look as I did then.

I hate each crease upon my face,
cover dark spots without a trace.
Imperfection means less than ten.
I have to be fifteen again.

Flawless skin, unmarred by age,
or life or pain or just plain rage.
The blood explodes the vessels and
I want to look as I did then.

I'll purchase anything I need;
believe all sophist books I read.
I will not, can not rest, my friend.
I have to be fifteen again.

And I do curse society
for making me hate little me.
Shallow, vain, I will pretend
to make myself fifteen again.

art abstract: picasso visited

One line
many lines
roll and rock lines
making guitar jokes!

a circle of swatches
soft challis
woven in paisley
jetties of energy!

cells
embryos
quarks
creating curves!

clusters of color
swirling in motion
dancing a guitar tune!

initiation

The smile escapes but rarely lasts on lips.
And eyes once bright grow dim from time to time.
With white sad face an empty void does mime
a broken heart and soul that madly slips
from light to dark. The mind takes hold and trips.
It captures thoughts into perceptive rhyme
to reconstruct the past scenes free of crime.
The play cannot end sweet with daggered whips.

Forget the past... a hell of microdots,
now scattered far beyond the time warp where
there is not time. If pen creates fresh plots
and reckons with sagacity once rare
to keep alive a chemistry of prayer,
then colored stars will light the sky with flare.

ancient rose

Looking out of the window I see
the swirling of snow on emptying streets
The stray cats are not there. No living things
in sight until morning when the sun will redden
the damp graying air.
The wind breathes hard and fast even at dawn.
Ancient rose-colored fingers stretch the sky,
the same pink sky as Romans watched.

The sky changes again, heavy with night breaths,
breaths softer than a sigh that lingers in your ear,
wind vibrations bending into space.
The trees do not move.
Again the north wind cries its swirling songs,
breaking stillness in wild aerobic gusts.

I leave my window seat thinking of summer
and scents of lilac and sea.
A mist of harbor fog, membraning above the bridge,
coats the same spear-branched trees
which glare now like an idle reminder
of drying bones that ash white.

special room on avenue d *(for mom)*

The triangular room was tight and crowded.
Its single window, abundant in light,
speckled shadows on the walls
through thin dotted-swiss curtains.
Boxes for storage and hidden novelties piled high
were transformed into sturdy wooden tables.
Chatty Cathy dolls were fed out of ancient cups
set on lace dollies.
Trunks became beds, freshly blanketed
with old velvet drapes
where those who dozed feigned sleep.

Tool boxes were heavy and laden
with remarkable jewels, treasures of a princess.
Discarded clothes were spun in gold thread
and carefully draped around me, a stunning model.
A pungent aroma of moth balls
accompanied each private fashion show.
Wondrous conversations and dialogues
between Ken and Barbie echo still.
On occasion, seminars were held.

The door was closed then behind me.
It is slightly ajar now and whispered giggles
invite the listeners to join the tea parties
again.

abba

Tonight through thin lips I call you, Father.
The wind interferes with our dialogue.
My breath upon the pane reveals the fog
outside, heavy, glazing the grass, farther
down the path past the ripe peach trees. Father,
does my voice sound muffled through the fog?
Fog horns remind me of a safari dialogue
between elephants and tigers. The farther
away they seem to blow, the farther
the danger will be, until finally the fog
will dissipate, the stark sun drying the fog.
Unless, of course, there is no sun, Father.
Perhaps, then, the moon will take over, Father.

chaos

When I feel the amber marble
and I rub it on my flesh;
when I kiss the black abyss
then I'll know its tattered mesh.

All along the rocks are jagged,
all across the whited land.
And the many pebbles havoc
reek and reel this furrowed mess.

Reek and reel with unknown panic.
Reek and reel with slithered bash.
Reek and reel with monstrous manic.
Peak and peal with untold crash.

Yes I hear the metered language
and I know it's forced, you see.
Yet, I have to hear the heartbeat,
And you'll see the imagery.

When you smell the yellow marble
and you throw it to the floor.
When you hear the muffled garble,
then you'll know its tattooed roar.

Bleeding red and all around
they're crying out in slivered pain;
crying out like little children
while the darkness hides the stain.

Red is black in nightmared vision
It is not the same at dawn
when the dying hope has marched in,
hope that is a constant pawn.

Pushing in a sea of danger,
pushing ever to the end,
pushing just to keep the wager,
pushing for a bartered bend.

Will it ever really end then?
Can the mind slow down to peace?
Can the earth regain composure
and a scheduled time release?